WORKING FROM HOME

The book is dedicated to Shirley May - founder of Young Identity, Rosie Stuart - Young People's producer at HOME and all the young creatives and artists involved, in the making of this book.

What is family?
It's found at the heart of HOME
Inspirational love

Haiku by Shirley May

FOREWORD

I first commissioned Young Identity to perform as part of HOME's first birthday celebrations in 2016. It was a captivating performance and the highlight of the programme that weekend. The raw, heartfelt poetry made the audience sit up and listen to the voices of these incredibly talented young writers. I knew I wanted to continue working with Young Identity from that day.

Since then we have welcomed hundreds of young people to weekly Young Identity writing workshops, commissioned several performances in response to the breadth of HOME's artistic programme including Carol Ann Duffy's politically charged play My Country: A Work in Progress, Phil Collin's major solo exhibition Can't Do Right for Doing Wrong and Noor Afshan Mirza and Brad Butler's fiction film installation The Scar. We've supported new work as part of PUSH Festival, hosted BBC's Words First and at the end of 2019 made Young Identity Resident Artists of HOME in recognition of their impact on Manchester's cultural landscape.

This book is a celebration of a wonderful partnership between HOME and Young Identity and one that I am personally extremely proud of. The outstanding poetry contained within these pages breathes life into the art on the walls, on the stages and in the cinemas of HOME, bringing fresh perspectives, energy and fire, fuelled by youthful passion, power and politics.

It was a real privilege to be asked to write the foreward for this book (although slightly terrifying when I know my mediocre writing will be followed by such exceptional poetry) as it is a privilege to be part of the Young Identity family.
I work with young people in order to be challenged, to unearth new talent, to champion unheard voices, to develop career opportunities and to offer creativity as a form of self expression and personal growth - everything that Young Identity stand for and promote in bucketfuls. I have recently become a mother and I can only hope that my daughter can be part of such a supportive and creative collective as Young Identity throughout her formative teenage years and into adulthood.

With the 5th birthday fast approaching, Young Identity are now at the forefront of HOME's programme and a firm fixture in the building. I am eternally grateful for the way Young Identity have informed my own work and for all of the poems, debates, laughs, tears, pizzas, crisps and biscuits we have shared since we first met.

Take the time with these poems that they deserve and enjoy every word.

Rosie Stuart
Young People's Programme Producer
HOME

WORKING FROM HOME

●●●●●

MY COUNTRY

A CURTAIN RAISER
PERFORMED 22 APRIL 2017

WRITTEN AND PERFORMED BY
FRANKIE BLAUS, IANTHE CORDINGLEY, DAMANI DENNISUR, ERIN DAWSON,
ROMA HAVERS, SCARLETT SUMMERS, REECE WILLIAMS, JONATHAN WILSON

DIRECTORS
DESIREE REYNOLDS AND NICOLE MAY

THE NATIONAL THEATRE PRESENTS: MY COUNTRY

THEATRE
18 APR 2017 - 22 APR 2017

(IN THE WORDS OF PEOPLE ACROSS THE UK AND CAROL ANN DUFFY)

In the days following the Brexit vote, a team from the National Theatre spoke to people nationwide, aged 9 to 97, to hear their views on the country we call home. In a series of deeply personal interviews, they heard opinions that were honest, emotional, funny, and sometimes extreme. My Country puts their words centre stage. Britannia calls a meeting, to listen to her people. The debate is passionate, stereotypes nailed and opinions divided.

Can there ever be a United Kingdom?

These real testimonials are interwoven with speeches from party leaders of the time in this ground breaking new play by Carol Ann Duffy, Poet Laureate and director Rufus Norris.

"WHAT IS ARTICLE 50 AND WHO WROTE THE OTHER 49?"

Young Identity explore 'My Country', post-Brexit, in a curtain raiser performance directed by Desiree Reynolds and Nicole May. Participants from Young Identity wrote in response to material gathered by the National Theatre for My Country (in the words of people across the UK and Carol Ann Duffy) and explored their own feelings following the referendum.

This short performance took place on stage before the evening and matinee performances of 'My Country' on Saturday 22 April 2017 and was re-performed on several occasions, including Hay Festival 2017.

Included here is an excerpt from the performance and poems from five of the eight writers.

MY COUNTRY

CONTENTS

I DON'T WANT MY COUNTRY BACK

This country had an absent father;
I am all the birthdays that were missed.
Childhood summers spent in countries where we drank oil
to wash away the acrid taste of foreign kids dreams.
Britain skipped school
to go looting at the abandoned wishing well; just wanted
to know if anyone bled fear the same colour as theirs.

Melancholy has long gone
stagnant in the pit of the well,
this Britain is a botched abortion
my grief birthed in a basement where vagrants dwell,
Britain has always been too in love with its own agony -
too busy pretending to converse with the moon
to worry about kids on street corners
growing old too soon, a degenerate realist:
Britain knows it can only offer more hollowness
to a man whose only lover has ever been
a lighter and a silver spoon.

Now, Britain is sweating in a too-big-suit,

wearing leg braces and nervously saving

her the last dance. Britain touches fingertips

with the ghost in the mirror.

This is a country woven from old thread,

but it feels as though these streets are still teething.

Ianthe Cordingley

BORROWED TIME

My country isn't exactly mine
I'm not quite trespassing more like squatting
on borrowed time—
and Brexit could well be Latin for eviction,
Article 50 has been served
after the operation.

Operation fraternise with Black folk
to mobilise the Black vote,
'Them' and 'us' and chartered boats to send
'them' back home.
Operation post-Brexit blues,
to find out if it's possible for melanin to bruise,
whitewash the truth into a post-racial myth,
xenophobic MPs taking pics with Ethnic kids,
does anybody really know what Brexit is?

Operation nose job,
Britannia narrowed the nose of her borders
to spite her face -
this would have Darcus Howling in his grave.

Reece Williams

BREXIT MEANS BREXIT

What is Brexit?
What is Article 50 and who wrote the other 49?
Real votes for real people?
What am I then? A ghost?
Since when did playground bullies start
running the country shouting *'stop hitting yourself!'*
as we punch ourselves in the face
with our own sovereignty?
Why is Farage anti-immigrant when he has a French
surname and a German wife?
Why do so many questions fill my head
when we just had a referendum to answer them?
Why are expats respected and immigrants aren't?
Why do people trust the Sun when they spat on the dead?

Has the truth died?
Who will go to her funeral?

Who has taken your country?
Mine is a boat slowly drowning.
Is the holocaust possible again
when men are no longer seen as men
but anonymous insects cowering under a banker's boot?
Since when are people swarms

and who is calling pest control?

When did we stop being great?

Will we only be able to look back on tragedy

and say "that shouldn't happen"

rather than stop it before it's too late?

Where is this 350 million?

Has the bus driven off the road?

Jonathan Wilson

NO ISLAND IS AN ISLAND

My country found itself on a Gap Year in India,
bought up all the ivory and shaved the tusks,
so we couldn't see their crux, a piano key for every hip,
for a wardrobe full of fur coats
and hareem pants they bought duty free.

My country taught its favourite recipe
to the ones who invented it, but left
the spices in the rack so they wouldn't remember it,
talked of stealing while picking pineapple
from between their teeth.

My country has a Napoleon Complex,
stabbed us in the back so we can't see
how short the knife is; loaded dice rolled
only zeroes, because they tippex'd out the black spots,
blamed our heart of darkness on a blood clot.

My country trades in Rosetta Stone,
so we'll forget the hieroglyphs,
just Caucasian cliffs, stained by tea thrown
from George's Mount, accounts dishonestly
in maps made bite sized for the GCSE

so we couldn't tell their red tracks
wiped on doormats,
so their shoes were clean
when they came home;
I didn't know our country always took its exit
before it could be traced
always took an amnesty
over being shamed or blamed the 'other'
for a history that was never taught;

I was sold short.

My country put sovereigns on coins
so we'd always know where the money went
but spent itself,
and forgot to tell me this story.

Roma Havers

TRANSCRIPT

"Who gave you permission to touch *my* things?
Come into *my* house and act like I don't know where the
knives are; cockroaches, rodents
Continue behaving I'm ignorant to pesticide we keep in the
basement
How can we keep the sheets clean when insects infest the
English nest'
Fermenting a plague enticing the black death
Then you dare to utter letters like NHS
I suggest you go learn the rest of the alphabet
You demons tried to infiltrate our gates
Bring me glimpses of Hell disguised as a peaceful protest,
give it a rest
Why do *I* have to live in hell when it's blatant Satan is
dodging immigration
Why is it becoming more and more difficult to differentiate
between human beings and mouldy trash
You should be glad we didn't kick you and your 40 kids off
the couch and benefits
I caught you stealing coins from the corner
Who gave you permission to touch *my* things?"

Damani Dennisur

WE

We, the people, so scared of honesty,
Lost without a clue what we are doing,
Begin to criticise the policy,
Before learning the truth of the ruling.

This country talks until words lose meaning,
Yet we are deaf when we are asked to choose,
Discover ignorance is not freeing,
Still, we turn our cheek to reason, to views

That contradicts those we'll never deny,
Deter change that disguises improvement,
Long for a past, that's rose-tinted with time,
Stultified yet satisfied it's proven

If we open ourselves to the answers,
We'll find more that unites than divides us.

Erin Dawson

OUR COUNTRY

The drug they force on
our shores: nostalgia. Hungry
hearts are prone to eating lies;
I would know: I'm starving. But, try
as they might, Brexit
will never resemble Trafalgar.

Why has the flesh of Christ changed
again? Why are Sunday Schools
handing out colouring books
made of The Messiah's skin,
already filled in, some pallid blend of
green and white?

Home is not what some papers claim is my birthplace.

I've made a statement without a resolution;
does that feel -
familiar?

Theresa May is writing the sequel to the King James Bible;
Prophets need no oversight, but England
Overnight I found my own answers
in the stifled gibberish

between your broadsheet ballot papers:
You sent Jesus back
to where he came from. You took my hymns,
and you turned them into racist pop songs.
England, you are not
plagued by a 2 point divide:
you are that divide.

Because while you argue about how you voted
as though every day isn't April 1st;
while you sit in Chorlton pubs
writing politically uninformed verse;
while you dress skeletons in platitudes like:
"mate, you see the thing about Brexit is
it could be better
but it could be a lot worse!"

Big-wigs in suits are
crowd-funding our country's hearse.

Frankie Blaus

THIS IS HUMAN: OCCUPY

LIVE PERFORMANCE
PERFORMED 29TH AUGUST 2017

WRITTEN AND PERFORMED BY
FRANKIE BLAUS, DAMANI DENNISUR, ROMA HAVERS, KAYLEIGH HICKS,
ISAIAH HULL, TOREH O'GARRO, HAAMID SHARIF

CONCEPT AND STAGING
ISAIAH HULL

A live performance from Young Identity responding to the sensory exhibition 'This Is Human', taking inspiration from the installation 'Atlas', conceived by Isaiah Hull.

THIS IS HUMAN: OCCUPY

EXHIBITION
9 AUG 2017 – 31 AUG 2017

Conceived by Isaiah Hull and the Project X artist collective, taking inspiration from the brain and the four main areas controlling emotion, movement, biological rhythm and sense, this innovative project *'This is Human'* combined sensory installations, live performances, interactive experiences and celebrations.

The gallery housed a continuous event, Occupy. A large-scale, interactive puppet built by Katy-Anne Bellis stood without identifying with age, sex or birthplace.

All that was known was its name, Atlas.

Ignoring the elitist culture of art venues and claiming the space as its own, the titan represented those who were not the casual gallery-goer. Almost in protest, Occupy worked with a wide range of artists throughout the weeks of August 2017 when Atlas was challenged, probed, praised and left to its own devices.

"HE IS TIRED OF YOU HUMANS - HE HAS GIVEN UP HIS GODS FOR LENT"

On 29th August 2017 poets from Young Identity performed poems in response to the exhibit, as part of the *'Funeral of Atlas'*; staged by Isaiah Hull.

CONTENTS

ALL GODS LIVE ON (BORROWED TIME)

When Atlas laughs
he is a wet dog shaking off the rain; right now
Atlas is crying outside the off licence again.

He is Stella-strong and Artois-charming,
barred from your everywhere
and turning Tartarus.

He has given up his gods for Lent,
he's emptied his cups,
blood-drunk from the leavings of the heaven sent,

because when it comes to creatures like us
a life is never the first thing to be seen.
If humans are made of stars their flags
are made of dead bodies.

He has read your bible,
knows all gods live on borrowed time,
knows the spine for the overly rehearsed line it is.

His ear, pressed against the pavement,
is that of a child's to the city's
shell, seldom
surprised at what is heard; all change saved for
the dried up

wishing wells; coins turning tail
the only thing he sees

as prophecy—rusted penny for a hand mirror—
he's crafting honesty with the left-overs
of your back pocket
coin slots for eye sockets, all he sees

the thick brown line
between what is golden, and what is true.

If men are made in the image of gods
take a look at Atlas:
what does that make you?

Frankie Blaus

THE PLEIADES

Before Atlas was Atlas
her name was Anonymous:
illegible in the corner of every map.
Now she authors with her toes alone,
runs in circles while the sun times her,
and fights the urge to discus
the basket-earth from her crown.

She births her first seven souls
with her knees split
and nurses them under its shadow.
She promises her daughters she feels no weight
knows her head's dents
so it rests well.
Now handicapped:
she teaches her daughters to keep
theirs free for bow and arrows.
Now, they circle her to keep the Gods out,
her only ring: the equator
welded to her scalp.
Callused from manual labour,

still chasing down the sun,
with her daughters
as their thighs
chafe and burn,
asthmatic at dusk:

mother you are too strong for us,
we weep with dizziness,
our arms ache when we
rise to touch your un-sweating brow,
and you feel nothing.

While we sleep,
she gathers the ocean from her fingertips
to imitate tears
and squeezes each toe
until they cramp,
feigns laughter until Hera joins her.

She's shocked that the planets orbit without her,
bare-headed, earth in lap,
cross-legged she teaches them nymphing:
to buckle oceans with their fists,
knuckle cities until they scrape the sky,
suckle mountains until they dribble sunset and ask:
Why can't we do this every day?

She didn't know to be mother
is to hold the earth without blinking,
and at the same time
tell the truth of your tiredness.

Roma Havers

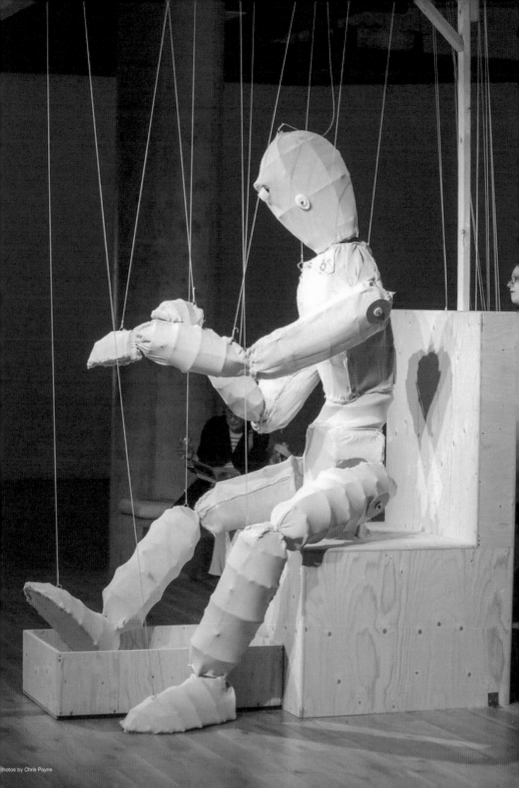

ATLAS

Every time Eos delivered dawn, Atlas
begged her birds to blind him.
He had enough of seeing the world
he was forced to protect,
for humans were once his servants,
offering respect so they may continue
with their feeble lives,
but once ripped his skin
as punishment for the Titan war,
strung him into the shadows of the clouds
and peeled away his power,
like a Pegasus plucked of its wings,
humans began to treat Atlas like a dirty toy.

There are times now when Atlas cries
hoping that the world notices his pain,
but he knows no one cares.

How dare you use him as a form of entertainment,
how dare you touch his limbs without permission,
how dare you smile when he cries and enjoy his misery
whilst sipping wine?
Who gave you the right to speak in his presence?

He's tired of you humans
reducing wonders of the world
into your playthings out of spite,

when you were once puppets yourselves to gods.

Toreh O'Garro

THE SCAR

EXHIBITION OPENING PERFORMANCE
PERFORMED 9 FEB 2018

WRITTEN AND PERFORMED BY
ROMA HAVERS, BILLIE MEREDITH, ELLA OTOMEWO

DIRECTOR AND FACILITATOR
NICOLE MAY

PRODUCER
ROSIE STUART

A live performance from Young Identity responding to the themes of Noor Afshan Mirza & Brad Butler's exhibition 'THE SCAR'.

NOOR AFSHAN MIRZA & BRAD BUTLER: THE SCAR

EXHIBITION
10 FEB 2018 – 2 APR 2018

"Together we are barrelling towards the scene of the accident at 120 kilometres an hour."

Noor Afshan Mirza and Brad Butler's fiction film installation weaves together conspiracy, gangster, noir, politics, crash theory, fantasy and reality into a disrupted narrative and genre exploration that ignites a gender revolution.

Across three chapters with the same characters that all end in a car crash, The Scar tells its story from the position of the female passenger, Yenge. Through her journey, we begin to address corrupt systems that hold power, explore ways to 'get out' of the car and begin to imagine an alternative society no longer dominated by patriarchy.

Noor Afshan Mirza and Brad Butler's work engages with contradictions of inequality, power, privilege and (non) participation. Their collaboration spans moving image, installation, workshops, sound, text and performed actions.

Differentiating between work made 'in' struggle and work made about struggle they take up an expanded notion of how to think politics with and through the body.

"JUSTICE IS NOT A BAG OF BONES — "IS IT POSSIBLE TO WOMAN ALONE?"

© Photos by Lee Baxter

The Scar is commissioned by FLAMIN Productions through FILM LONDON Artists' Moving Image Network with funding from Arts Council England in partnership with HOME & no.w.here with support from àngels Barcelona, Centre national des arts plastiques France, Delfina Foundation, Edith-Russ-Haus Germany, London College of Communication, Razwana Akram, Spectre Productions and University of Salford Art Collection

THE SCAR

CONTENTS

OUTLIER

Born with umbilical-ed wrists to prove
she birthed herself:
cursed-hand-dealt
as placenta dried.
Mother: wishful-welling at the closed eye.

Many daughters have been well-thrown (unwished)
or bucket-dipped,
until their body is an Achilles Heel and their ankle a fore-
fingered promise,
since her distress is not a damsel but an apricot -
stoned yet unblemished. She never claimed womanhood
in the collective sense,

woman-ed lonely as a lioness when her pride
unprouds itself.
Too often sisters hoodwink the unassigned,
and find a tribe in diatribing othered-women.
Is it possible to woman alone?
People under glass ceilings should throw stones.

Roma Havers

but bones to kill the dead

RESISTANT DEAD

They lie in the underside of limbo,
between the sheets of our plains,
inhaling whispers like an almost existence.
Last words in vocal chords,
cross wrists in a flight-like fashion.

The lost cannot be buried.
Hallowed and underfoot,
memories embalmed and stagnant,
the myths of these lives live longer
than the winds they're carried on.

The swollen spines of women's resistance,
cracked sternum and throat,
swallowed in belt-buckled 4 door rooms,
hallucinations of green-lit shoulder-guilted,

Faces pressed, distorted against our aftermath,
palms printed, clammy fate lines on the insides
of the in-between.
Throats up-chuck in the heaving of man-made ghosts,
torsos lurched in the echo rhythm of last breaths.

Legend is impenetrable.
Resistance of the perished,
sing on the underside of limbo.

Billie Meredith

UNBREATH

I know I carry memory in my body,
but I think it has forgotten how to dance.
My lungs are mirrors of each other -
growing wildflowers
that long to stretch out of
my mouth in thanks for breath.

I feel like I have to be willow tree strong,
measuring my wisdom by tree-ring dating,
forgetting that I would have to be
cut through first.

I wish I knew how to speak without words.

I am normally a quiet person.
Abandoning sleep
because I think Night would be lonely without me.
I'm losing myself in keeping up appearances,
and I don't want to be painted as a Madonna.
You don't need to smooth over my flaws,
I'd rather be disfigured in grace.
And see, my tongue is a flint stone
and against my steel lips
it sets houses on fire.

Ella Otomewo

THE SCAR

Hallowed and underfoot, cracked sternum and throat.
It is impossible to lose one person at a time.
Maybe the state dug graves to swallow men.
Is it possible to woman alone?

Some other doorstep is missing the knuckles of a
daughter - anonymous is less a threat of no-named than
no-listened, they were always more a body of words than
a state of work,
'Justice is not a bag of bones'
but you can't make a wishbone of the human clavicle,
you can't circumference a life in a lesion of wrist
you can't identify a body if you didn't know it alive,
have you ever seen a naked skeleton before?
a knuckle bleached with fight,
mounted like the head of a boar.

We're always too long in the look
too short in the listen,
I always wanted to be more than a blank page
- to wring an inkwell from another's knuckle,
to disappear into anonymous by name-loss alone,
not in act
not in purpose.

I would take a lifetime of bad luck
for a house-full of cracked mirrors and roomful of listen:
to be gossiped upon in the original sense
to secret well enough to be a threat.
'If it looks like a miracle it was'
because people were craving one'
but I prefer an unmanned fire and a long-listened woe.

It is impossible to lose one person at a time.
Maybe the state dug graves to swallow men.
Is it possible to woman alone?
Hallowed and underfoot, cracked sternum and throat.

Knuckle-bloodied vision in a red dress,
I too have ripped myself from barked frame.
These sat-camped rounded confessionals,
the un-rooted ripping of herself post-gossip,
hemless militia, crimson in intentions with rip-claw
hindsight.
Neck owns the imprints of back-seat precious stones;
there is a charge in the eyeing of scars.

I've often found myself tacked less to women-hoods
in want of a circumcised peripheral.
In fired shadows pain is flicker-lit and tortured.
This round is the remnant of a half-empire's hearing.

Here our words are sacred in tongue,
phonetic crucifixion in silence
lullabies and war songs sound the same when alight.

  Maybe the state dug graves to swallow men
  Is it possible to woman alone?
  Hallowed and underfoot, cracked sternum and throat
  It is impossible to lose one person at a time

Maybe the state dug graves to swallow men.
and the soil exhaled a sunken story too thin to catch with
the naked eye.
She was a petri dish of her family's forgotten truths and
remembered lies.

When they fought each other, breathless;
they listened for the first time.
With every hit they understood a little more
about why they were there.
She reclaimed blue blood as the way stories were
inked under her skin.
A swelling, blue bloodied bruise perches under
the sleeve of a red dress.
She was cloaked in stale sweat and faithfulness
to a cause that the state hoped to burry with her gossip.
Gossip: a tarnished word meaning to gather,

together round a camp-fire and swap switch-blade stories
and secrets of uprising.

Is it possible to Woman alone?
Hallowed and underfoot, cracked sternum and throat.
It is impossible to lose one person at a time.
Maybe the state dug graves to swallow men.

Is it possible to woman alone?

Roma Havers, Billie Meredith, Ella Otomewo

IF YOU'RE GONNA DO IT DO IT RIGHT: TOGETHER

EXHIBITION OPENING PERFORMANCE
PERFORMED 9-30 AUG 2018

WRITTEN AND PERFORMED BY
NASIMA BEGUM, FRANKIE BLAUS, ROMA HAVERS, KAT HUMPHREY, BILLIE MEREDITH, TOREH O'GARRO, NAOMI SAMPSON

DIRECTORS
NICOLE MAY & SHIRLEY MAY

PRODUCER
ROSIE STUART

INTRODUCTIONS
ISAIAH HULL & JARDEL RODRIGUEZ

A live performance from Young Identity responding to the themes of Phil Collins' exhibition 'Can't Do Right For Doing Wrong'.

PHIL COLLINS: CAN'T DO RIGHT FOR DOING WRONG

EXHIBITION
7 Jul 2018 – 16 Sep 2018

Phil Collins. 'Can't Do Right For Doing Wrong' features three large-scale installations – *'Ceremony, 'my heart's in my hand, and my hand is pierced, and my hand's in the bag, and the bag is shut, and my heart is caught' and 'Delete Beach'* – which use digital and analogue technologies to tell the stories of individuals and social groups living under late, accelerated disaster-capitalism.

Bringing together works from the last five years, the exhibition is an expansive spatial and poetic statement which invites engagement with the voices and perspectives of the homeless, the future of resistance in a world without fossil fuels, and the life and revolutionary work of Friedrich Engels whose insights into the 19th century injustices continue to reverberate in today's society.

"WE ARE OIL SLICKS OF POSSIBILITY — MIDNIGHT PRAYERS"

Manchester's finest poetry collective Young Identity responded to Phil Collins' 'Can't Do Right For Doing Wrong' with a series of newly commissioned pieces reflecting on the politically driven themes of this extensive exhibition. After a month of immersing themselves in the artwork, the poets performed pieces inspired by the three major works in the exhibition; 'Ceremony, 'my heart's in my hand…' and 'Delete Beach' in and around HOME throughout August.

For this performance, Young Identity responded to the exhibition themes as a whole, which touch on everyday hardships, struggles and solidarity seen through various forms of popular culture.

IF YOU'RE GONNA DO IT RIGHT DO IT TOGETHER

CONTENTS

IF YOU'RE GONNA DO IT RIGHT: WORK

PERFORMED 9 AUG 2018

'Ceremony' centres the work and legacy of Friedrich Engels, co-founder of communist theory with his friend Karl Marx who lived here for 20 years.

The 1917 Russian Revolution shaped the political landscape of the 20th century. But it was in Manchester, not Imperial Russia, that the idea of communism was born, developed in large part through Engels' ideas which were shaped by what he observed in the world's first industrial city. Through the complex layering of a decommissioned 1970 statue from Eastern Europe, a public gathering, a television documentary, and a new gallery film, Collins' multi-faceted project links Engels' work to the social conditions of Britain today.

Presented exactly one year after the statue of Engels was inaugurated outside HOME, where it remains as a permanent

'Ceremony' was co-commissioned by 14-18 NOW, HOME, Manchester and Manchester International Festival. Produced by HOME, Manchester, Manchester International Festival, Shady Lane Productions and Tigerlily Productions. Supported by Arts Council England's Ambition for Excellence, the BBC, the Henry Moore Foundation and My Festival Circle. 'Ceremony' also tours to Baltic, Gateshead, Fri 22 Jun – Sun 30 Sep; MAC, Belfast, Thu 9 Aug – Sun 28 Oct 2018; and Cooper Gallery, Duncan of Jordanstone College of Art and Design, University of Dundee, Thu 18 Jan – Sat 16 Feb 2019.

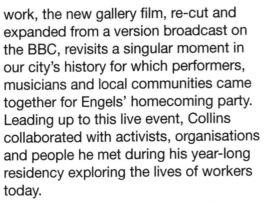

work, the new gallery film, re-cut and expanded from a version broadcast on the BBC, revisits a singular moment in our city's history for which performers, musicians and local communities came together for Engels' homecoming party. Leading up to this live event, Collins collaborated with activists, organisations and people he met during his year-long residency exploring the lives of workers today.

Part of 14-18 NOW, the UK's arts programme for the First World War, 'Ceremony' reconnects Manchester to the idea of communism, which transformed the post-war world and continues to provide a visionary alternative to the tyranny of capital which governs our political, economic and emotional lives.

WHAT IS CEREMONY?

Origin Latin – 'caeremonia'

the practice of preservation
the practice of encapsulation

Remembrance,
tradition
the practice of legacy
Continuity,

the practice of sacred observance
a solemn public or state occasion

an Officiation,
a religious event
Rituals,
Rites,
the practice of celebrating
a meaningful gesture

an Honorarium,
the royal assent
What is Ceremony?
a formality.

Nasima Begum, Billie Meredith

THE NOTION OF HOME

Of intense freedom coated in reds of a hard-fought idea,
a statue with waistline unforgivable, a marble bleed.
They made a forget-me-not of his torso,
scar healed in theory alone,
context has all calling here.
Birthplace of theory,
of system, of social organization,
community property, of needs and ability
Communism is coming home.
Engels crawls back to his prides, his joys,
our polygot posterboy, reedless fencer
to stone himself against the breast of our
unelected leaders,
from field to foredoor

Who are the scarecrows supposed to pray to now?
Strawman no longer,
20 leagues of a life man's movement,
of a near death democracy
and a bourgeois war-less status quo choking two years.
In the aftermath of an uninformed public
and a poet's opinion,
are the greys for a sickle celled revolution.
Socialists with ballpoint pens -
we have nothing to lose.

Billie Meredith

THE 99

99 ways to gerrymander
the redrawing of
repackaged opinion
sever the literates

the outliers
the unspent
99 new votes that will never matter
99 senate counts that never saw paper

the 99 are
43 million still on food stamps
philately lacking working members
each slip sold for a 'many more'

99 £16,000 less savings
sharehouse of 6
lacking a life of our own
6 more mouths of a broken system

7.3% fumbling in persistent poverty
yet resistant to anarchic theologies
blunt on the forearms of England
God save the first world

another 5 million we can call unclothed
52% with abandonment issues
for a sad bent-lipped island barely out the door
48 (too many foreign luxuries and fell in love) %

87% of Germans didn't vote for an 'Alternative'
in 1932% did
held lisps for an Austrian painter
whose name slips my moral compass

"99% is a myth
and the '1%' is likely to err
on the low side"

but the 99 had
951 cities
85 countries

and a movement
an occupation
of a failed percentile
of a revolution
found 99 more ways to self-hail

Billie Meredith

IF YOU'RE GONNA DO IT RIGHT: SAFE

PERFORMED 16 AUG 2018

'my heart's in my hand, and my hand is pierced, and my hand's in the bag, and the bag is shut, and my heart is caught' is a project from 2013 developed in collaboration with guests of GULLIVER Survival Station for the Homeless, located under the railway arches at Cologne's central station. Selected material from over a thousand free and anonymised phone calls recorded at the facility was posted to a group of international musicians, serving as the starting point for original new tracks presented in the exhibition as 7" vinyl records in a series of specially designed listening booths.

The contributors included some of Collins' personal heroes (Scritti Politti, David Sylvian, Lætitia Sadier, Damon & Naomi), trailblazing experimental acts (Demdike Stare, Planningtorock, Maria Minerva, Pye Corner Audio, Heroin In Tahiti, Peaking Lights),

'my heart's in my hand...' was originally produced for 'In Every Dream Home a Heartache', a solo exhibition at Museum Ludwig Cologne (2013). Supported by Akademie der Künste der Welt.

Cologne musicians across different generations (Elektronische Musik aus: Köln, Pluramon, Cologne Tape), and a special guest turn by the German indie superstar Julia Hummer.

Bringing to the fore the lyrical potential of the human voice when it stands in for subjects of city life who are purposely ignored and routinely overlooked, 'my heart's in my hand…' dramatises the moment of communication as an intimate and ambivalent exchange. The installation gains a special resonance in Manchester where homelessness is at an all-time high, particularly in tandem with 'Ceremony' and its unorthodox look at the realities of life in 21st century austerity Britain.

TOREH

Dear so-called humans:
my name is Toreh, Toreh and Toreh,
one of them is correct,
and the other I accept,

England couldn't give a damn today.

Even though I was born in it's birthplace,
I've struggled to talk proper,
not the snooty English, rather
the conversational.
I'm still adjusting to your standard,
your proud invention of language
like 'thank you' can be both a positive
and negative response,
but it depends on the sarcasm,
and I'm not human for understanding that.

Don't you dare call me a monster.

My lettered introduction was too formal.
To seem socially acceptable
I've been switching between mediums,
you want a man to mirror you in conversation,
not reflect a challenge,
so never did I fidget in conversation

I didn't want to seem a bore,
but dozens were thrown that I was a little robot,
so I sent back an angry fist-filled message,
but my ears still couldn't understand the rules,
so more punches were sent on a right hook,
I was classified as a well-oiled machine.

Don't you dare call me a monster.

The teachers told me to express differently,
new method: I had to fax or write
each incident and feeling,
with the promise that each paper would be burned,
but when the big meetings came,
stacked papers from my mind were shared,

see I thought a promise is a promise
but they tore that contract too many times and finally
kicked me out,
a messenger of Hermes thrown off the delivery van
and given a letter that he doesn't belong.

Don't you dare call a monster.

I lost my skill to hold conversation,
so I shadowed the man in the mirror,
let him become our identity,
we practised faces,

like the happy one and the sad one,
and... and the empathy one...
I don't know how to show it though,
but I've been more in tune with it.
My psychiatrist would answer the pager to let me talk...
just talk...
trial and error strung my words together,
I was a little rusty on the conversational formula.
Shadows aren't meant to speak,
so I had to accept proverbs as an ally,

threw up a white flag to 'water under the bridge'
had to ride its ripples to be acceptable,
I may be allergic to fish,
but humans expect everyone to swim together.

Don't you dare call me a monster.

I've gone over enough years:
thirteen of the twenty-one,
I'm still Toreh but able to civilise better now,
sent a telegram to my past-self about a month ago,
telling him to be silent
and listen to our heart's inner Morse Code:

'I am not a monster, I am not a monster'

Toreh O'Garro

BODY LANGUAGE

As a child, I would plant
myself atop a tidal fingertip
and with shell-pressed ear, decant
all the ocean wished for only me to hear - which
I carry now as an MP3
the shanty that will one day deafen me

SAY IT

We've all sung to dogs, all pawed for the moon
like the ocean do - no, does! All rain
danced home with water in our socks, before
leaving our wet-work to the room

SAY IT

We've all blown smoke signals at bedroom windows

SAY IT

Through that screen, everything looks
so small. The twinkling of an 'I'
viewed as a hole is enough to pass
through any wall - and we have sought diamonds
with a drill-bit

SAY IT

Acquit all wild goodbyes
where bodies such as mine form habits
of happenings, canalside - drinking street fires
like a stale river, or loitering
in the Thames - a glass bottle waiting
to become a kaleidoscope of fragmentary "and-then's"

SAY IT

I am loading my flare gun with the tongue
of a lover: a warning shot against the night
when your body dove into mine, much like
the sky bruise of summer is swallowed
by the ocean when it tires of light -

my waters do not
ripple, but pucker to kiss the clouds
for filling their bodies to the brim
each and every night -

the distribution
of a tide perfectly embodies the flutter of a butterfly
permanently occupying clear skies
by thrashing: air particles flee and huddle
together for safety

SAY IT

Water assumes the shape of whatever houses it
moving into water is a commitment to breaking it –
I wish I could be honest

SAY IT

You are the space between my bedroom walls
and me - a fluttering, puckering
heartbeat, echo locating in the darkreach
the bubbles of air that I can and cannot
breathe. I wish I could be honest

SAY IT

I'm still smoking joints in a butcher's closet
lacking
the courage or the trust to feed
the both of us - I wish I could be honest

SAY IT

I'm sat here filleting fish
pocketing the guts
arranging viscera like a promise.

Frankie Blaus

IF YOU'RE GONNA DO IT RIGHT: EARTH

PERFORMED 23 AUG 2018

'Delete Beach' is an anime set in the near future which tells the story of a schoolgirl who joins an anti-capitalist resistance group in a society in which carbon-based energy is outlawed.

The film proposes a scenario describing the decline of the oil economy, with the prosperity of the boom years expiring and the necessity of infrastructural changes looming large. As an art form, anime has repeatedly addressed political themes, often through the lens of complex female characters.

In 'Delete Beach', a curious paradox is at work: society has reached an advanced state of independence from carbon fuels, yet it continues to toil as before under a regime of oppression, inequality, and control.

'Delete Beach' was commissioned by Bergen Assembly. Supported by Vestnorsk Filmsenter. Co-produced with HAU Hebbel am Ufer Berlin through funding provided by the German Cultural Foundation.

Following anime's recognisable aesthetic and storytelling strategies, Collins' collaboration with STUDIO4°C, one of Japan's leading animation studios 'Tekkonkinkreet', and pop auteur and film composer Mica Levi 'Under the Skin', 'Jackie' brings to life a world at once familiar and disquietingly corroded.

For the installation at HOME, 'Delete Beach' is conjured up as an apocalyptic, melancholy shoreline, crashing in from another dimension to play host to a dream-like animation environment.

DELETED BEACH

I wrote you waves in HTML.
Coded your name in,
the way it was spelt pixelated a shell of the people we
were
when deep purple was perfect
and each urchin would worship
we'd sleep early through curfew
while we drowned in a hologram.

Fortune found us on holiday
Palm trees on the strip (miss Penelope Pink)

//firewall.fullstop

Who was the felon who looked better in mink?
With a pocket full of rings that we had weddings in once...

All of my memory's gone.

I left your locket in the nook of an anemone once,
at least I think so.
All of my memory's gone.

Erm...

Azure, stained glass of casa da Celibate Nun.
We meet in secret on deleted beach whenever you're
drunk-

Where all of our messages are sent in bottled form
In hopes that Pirates don't find them beneath the eye of
this torrent storm.

Jardel Rodrigues

PLASTIC BEACH

an analog anemone
auto immutiny, techie told me
talk to frank
a dotted w
when I walked the plank
hash key halibut head
like shower sex
like floundering when I found her dead
like the compubox full of coral
reefer model
rolling me some sticky
keys quaaluded qwerty
amphetamine w/ Amphitrite
an analog anemone
Atlantis full of Apple Mac
dark webbed feet duckling dance
speckled searches not showing
on the bill
heartless feed them sunken lance
conditioned to terms like 'nigger' online
some worms
holier unseen
I capsized in teenage, tumble-dried in tumblr page
second eye crying like Nirnroot baby

black markets deep in the beached whale
bitcoin for blubber
for your molly jaw
spent seven years inside
porno hungry piranha on a fishing hook,
they pop-up
add
the whiff of blood
I over'bated
the seagulls go viral with what they steal from me.

blue drown. muted, left
unread
see the message in your bottle thaw
frozen phishing emails found
analog in anemone
an age of circus cubed in Ice Capades
deep sea tundra
torrent pirate bay

waterboard the firefox
and wear its pelt   dare to melt
and wear its pelt   dare to melt
and wear its pelt.   dare to melt.

Isaiah Hull

CAN'T DELETE WHAT IS UNDONE

We are oil slicks of possibility.
Moving with the rhythm of sundown's drums
and midnight prayers,
dancing in black, blue, purples and reds.
We are sediments of yesterday,
today and tomorrow's history
but bought like factory-borne amenities,
only useful for household chores.
Our bodies are not currency:
lottery tickets we pay forever to own,
just to lose ourselves again.
Sometimes, emancipation means death
because in dying they can no longer count the last pennies
of our breath.
What is it that we've been living for?
Because governments work us so we can buy comfortable
coffins
and leave legacies in payslips,
whilst our planet dies
on carbon monoxide highs
and malnutrition in fossil fuel shackles.
It is turning into a wasteland.
We were meant to be Earth's keeper,
having dominion over her gateways

and grasslands.
Watching evolution
create new species
with each turn of a century,
but now all that is left is
cemeteries at forest floor beds,
and an ozone,
thinning to mirror a crescent moon,
unable to shield us within.
The sun shines from Manchester skies
where once only rain slept,
and yet they swear that global warming is a hoax,
fabricated to hold us down in fear;
but we workers are left worn out from their
conveyor belt of lies.
I cling onto the hope that
revolution will choke this out,
But undeniably the damage has already been done.
She has martyred herself for freedom.
She didn't have nine lives.
Just one.
And we wasted her.
Spent our days
filling her embankments with
the pollution of our greed and mistrust.
We were all immigrants to her soil

and she welcomed us in,

she didn't build walls to keep us out

or prisons to keep us in,

we did that to ourselves.

And as the planets align,

forming allegiances against us for their own protection,

Mars looks gleeful in conspiracy,

that humans never touched his peaks

because he knows that his fate

would have been the same.

A galaxy of burning bodies

left voiceless and void.

Maybe we should have listened to those crazed

communists when they told us to stop,

let her breathe,

let her live.

Stop.

Leave her be.

Leave your sin.

Please,

stop,

she's stopped breathing.

Naomi Sampson

BURNER

Take my body and crumble the pieces until it's ash.

I'm asking you to burn whatever is left,

it's out of my control now.

I don't want to be misused anymore.

I was a broken puzzle piece being forced into shape,

strangled and cut as if I was piece of meat.

Your venom intoxicated my goodwill,

as if me wanting to do better was unsatisfactory.

My heart aches longing for what we should have been,

I took the world at my fingertips and spoke softly.

You told me to wash my mouth out,

told me to care about finer things.

I'll take what you crave and inject it inside of me,

it's the only way to make you listen.

The sheer waste is a powerful sign,

the manifestation of destruction is a beauty in itself,

so take my body and crumble the pieces until it's ash,

delete my existence as if I was never here,

because I don't want to be part of this world:

a world whose shattered veins are full of hostility,

hearts of resentment,

because at this moment in time

the mind is the epicentre of chaos,

and we are unified in this pandemonium.

Kat Humphreys

IMPRINT

PUSH FESTIVAL 2019
PERFORMED 22 JAN 2019 – 23 JAN 2019

WRITTEN AND PERFORMED BY
FRANKIE BLAUS, DAMANI DENNISUR, ROMA HAVERS, KAYLEIGH HICKS,
BILLIE MEREDITH, NAOMI SAMPSON, HAAMID SHARIF AND JAWARA TAIT

DIRECTOR
COURTNEY HAYLES

ASSISTANT DIRECTOR
KAT HUMPHREYS AND NICOLE MAY

PRODUCER
REECE WILLIAMS AND SHIRLEY MAY

COSTUME
SIDNIE COUTURE

IMPRINT

THEATRE
22 JAN 2019 - 23 JAN 2019

Imprint is an honest and introspective exploration of humanity, using poetry and theatre.

Shaped around the experiences that have brought us to this place, the poets of Young Identity rhapsodise about parents, absence and mental health, as they do their very best to shed snakeskin and grow past their trauma. Young Identity return following their sell-out show Hatch Home at Push Festival 2018.

Encapsulating the spirit and essence of Manchester, with metaphor and rhythmic performance, Imprint brings the city's finest and most fierce poets to centre stage.

"Once again HOME stand out from the crowd with their unique performances... The cast of Imprint take the idea of performing poetry and turn it into something utterly moving." – A Younger Theatre

"A refreshing ensemble performance... A highly charged, emotionally intelligent offering that simply made me want to rewind and experience it all again." – North West End on Hatch Home

© Photos by Rikki Chan

IMPRINT

CONTENTS

INTRO

IMPRINT

Ensemble

Husk: the outline of gone bodies,

effigy lines and holes, empty

genes: just a spiral of codes,

make up made up

like prosthetic limbs

we are part them,

Ellis, please know that I wrote this in the hope

that you would never understand,

you and I aren't,

we aren't the same:

idiosyncrasies fossilised in

finger-beds and smiles,

accents much thicker than ancestors

and inaccessible to grandma's ears,

shape-shifting like face marks,

your smile is part mine,

my name is merely the shell, inside is the pearl,

I am the veil, happiness is the face,

legacy and parentage are utter bullshit,

people are so desperate to attach

meaning to their lives,

when you're older you'll understand

why woodpeckers give themselves headaches

and why we don't name earthquakes,

dormant like a volcano

waiting for my time:

Dad's jacket never fits

but I imagined it would someday.

empty boxes always empty boxes

SHEDDING SNAKESKIN

I'm tryna shed the snakeskin hatched from shelly casing
sad attempts at changing only make space for the same
thing—I'm seeking refuge from Satan. We used to make
patterns in the sand, a luxury we had before Wall Street
bought the coastline. We moulded palaces with play doh
and held hands before they got rid of colour—they got
rid of summer before I was old enough to see it, stole
me from fellow hunters and bound my wrists and feet,
chopped my soul to pieces—threw the bits to hungry
demons, they tamed my tongue to diagnose me dumb—
wet my toes with spirits and set alight the rum.
I danced to out the flames, they blocked my throat with
guns and drowned the sound of my choking with rhythms
from old skin drums.

I spent every night reliving my vivid death. The killing
subsides with sunrise I can't remember last time I slept.
If I didn't sing the songs I was risking my morning breath
and when mornings my only friend I fear the fruits of
meeting sunset.

I learnt if you stay awake long enough all the days become
one. Laces of reality relax until undone, hieroglyph carved

dualities tattoo truth in spiral thumbs—it wrote itself into
my DNA. My soul dispelled to the trees today, it ran away
and my feet followed, chest hollowed.

    I searched the forest for something to fill the hole as
Babylon burns behind me I shower in lost control
and the trees whisper
    happiness is here if you want it
it shimmers gold as the hornet
a bed I can lieall will be alright
        I bleed venom into the sarcophagus
it calls out to a lot of us
    happiness is here if you want it
I answer
lie in a fancy coffins and forget the world hath happened
    happiness is here if you want it
    I hear you I trust you

I step inside the coffin stripping stacks of dead skin the
world which I was lost in will never see me again I figured I
could find some answer here or lose myself

but never worry now close the casket

                    Damani Dennisur

ACT 1: SELF

Happiness is here if you want it,
conveniently shelf-ridden, finger-tipped
in almost gold, lost in self-made mazes,
we bleed our way through paperweights.
How do we write a coming of age story
for the end of days?

Billie Meredith

I DON'T KNOW WHERE I AM

I don't know where I am

> *I wrote this poem on*
> *the back of a postcard*
> *it knows where I am*
> *better than I do*

Who am I? Who are you? Who is we?
Humanity is a self-contained identity.
We are born in the image of goodness,
yet born godless,
kids of reckless lineage,
growing into our trauma and wearing it 'til adulthood,
then passing it to our womb-borns,
in hand-me-downs and regrets,
and we wonder why our parents are here, tearless and
fistful,
or why they walk and speak as they do.

> *Name: Mara Jechonia*
> *Year of birth: 1997*
> *Birthplace: Jerusalem*

You look at me, funny,

as if you feel the same,

>*but one of us runs,*
>
>*whilst the other stays put.*

 You are not me,

and I, I am not you.

>*No one taught us to love what is different*

So I loved you, woman

all the same,

but pastor said I'm making an idol of self in your temple,

so again I retreated to the darker corners of my cell

and locked it up,

this poison that doesn't purge from my veins.

I tried to seek solace in my own body, but all I found was

dry bones, breathless.

We are taught that we cannot love till our capacity for

loving self is at least half full,

but self-love never defined the limits of you ever receiving

it in the first place.

No amount of self-loathing could ever warrant you to a life

of lonely.

But it's true- no hands could possibly heal you more than

your own.

So love your black.

Your skin is not brittle or bitter in its Saharan reds and

midnight blues.

you are sundew

A medias touch.

Your hair isn't a lamb for the sheer slaughter,

nor a crown because it does not equate your value

It is not your glory.

your thighs are not the guardian of your worth,

what lies between them cannot be undone from you

so move their hands now,

their bullets aren't your death warrant Their guns shall not

be put on you.

Name: John Whitting
Year of birth: 1978
Birthplace: Croydon

A lifetime of learning

and unlearning:

of willingness to step over knife edge

to take up space

beyond a burn spot

of identity that is created outside of all of this mess

and allowed to be made and rearranged over and over again

to throw up,

their words and my mother tongue

have brought me to the end -

to my final surrender,

but this time it is not to them,
this time it's to self.

So whilst we place our tears and frustrations
in bottles and jars,
lined up on our windowsills.
Recognise that the hatred and fear,
is not ours
it does not serve us.
We raise our bats and begin.

Name: Mine
Year of birth: Today
Birthplace: Here

Naomi Sampson

FRAME

Have you ever felt elbowless
when armlength held?
or shoulderless with no
nook for neck to settle?

Have you ever felt suddenly
unopposable and apish –
that finger-thumb stuck
like a penknife in fold?

Have you ever felt marked
by the punctuation of a hairline?
Or braced by the gristle under
a thumbnail like it might never get out?

Have you ever felt your skin
was just a filmy residue
that could be flensed
like a riddled wallpaper?

Have you ever felt enoughless
or like enough might be the wrong word?
Have you ever felt like a clothes hanger –
becoming less when swaddled,

and looking too much like absence
when baring its clavicle –
that metal bone –
hanged and hangable?

Have you ever felt like a white lie
when your mother phoned
'they say you're only as happy
 as your unhappiest child'

Have you ever felt like your body
was responsible for the enoughlessness
of a mirror - and wanting
to be found beautiful:
like a surfacing
not a digging-for.

Still enough is temporary, that's it's beauty.

                                        Roma Havers

EMPTY MEN

I see glass men and moths die, they fell out the skies. I
didn't kill them! Clouds of ash, grey teeth consume green
flesh, I never knew myself. Petrol fumes torch my head,
ricin seeps into chest, eluding death with every breath.
Lilin's sleep with me—I never questioned them.
I daydreamed Aphrodite, and asked the sun for direction
then we never spoke again. All my fingers have rings,
I have a chest with diamonds in, but still can't tell you why

empty men cover themselves in pretty things

Who am I! Consumed by doubt, the edge of the world is
a waterfall. Drowning in Diazepam, floating in Fluoxetine,
I lost certainty, voices ring in my head like a carousel,
I speak to duppies and Jezebels. They whisper about
journeys on sugared boats, sinking I see figures that look
like me, buried them wearing a mask of apathy, saw
fantasy in forgotten memories, drank bush wine until I saw
Anansi. He had all kinds of stories, but could not tell me
who I was, written in unremembered mother tongue.
He doesn't know me. I don't know me. I just did as told,
made runes for widowed queens, noosed the moon for
felicity. I was water in the Dead Sea.

Jawara Tait

WOLVES II

I'm not asleep, and yet my wolves are.
Their snores have brought the fireflies out tonight. It's not
calming, but it's not painful either. They're content.
They blink for the smaller invasions; life questions, inner
monologues, miniature searchings of self.

The lights have no intention, they just float, pulsing back at
me, gracefully whirling in and out of one another.
As though afterthoughts have come to gather, to debate
their importance in a random order.

The wolves are sleeping tonight.
For which I am grateful.
Yet it's strange to say they can be missed.
Stillness can still be unsettling.
These louds leave umami in the throat.

Billie Meredith

FOR ELLIS

With stories, there are choice many starting points.

mistakes make

page turners, so good men find themselves fatal

with voice.

Edit your life sentence until

it's perfect. Remember: Nothing

travels father-like starlight, so

the opinions of men are trite

cosmic dust, swirling in the nothing-night, as we sit,

comfortable, atop

our thrones of story: the self-made

sovereigns of our own Lifes glory

Frankie Blaus

MY MOTHER'S PRAYER

Our mother, who art in heaven and within me,
hallowed be our name.
Kings be done.
I am not Eve,
Adam is outdated as the Son.
On this earth, I shall find heaven,
in nobody's eyes but mine.
So today, I give you this bread,
once battered and bruised,
now transformed in my likeness.
I ask you for forgiveness,
for allowing Judas' their trespass,
upon my Holy ground.
As I forgive them,
for their attempts to foil my Eden,
and create Gethsemane within me.
But now you shall find me,
wholly delivered from their evil.
No longer within their graves—but risen.
No longer hanging as strange fruit on cursed fig trees,
withered like the bodies of my daughters
at the feet of Boaz—but free.
For mine is the kingdom,
the power,
and glory,
for ever, and ever.

A-woman.

Naomi Sampson

SELF-SOVEREIGN

I found my crown in your discomfort, taking everything

you claimed I lack: tragic Majesties my maker knows

you dream to have,

and I crafted

royalty. You said I

was born with parts missing; I hereby

decree: I was born the blueprint

to Divinity.

Frankie Blaus

ME AND THE BRAVE NEW WORLD

My hands are shivering above the styrofoam cup. My name is concealed as a reference number or student ID, if I'm lucky my name is simply mispronounced, misspelt. *'Miss, I want to know your first name.'*, I asked in school. Miss Carey looked after me, so her every detail mattered to me.

So how am I supposed to believe the government cares for me, when they don't even know my name? Unless they see a search for a terrorist in my internet history like ISIS, Al-Qaeda or Sinn Fein, but they'll let you get away with paedophilia, if you don't believe me, why don't you ask the BBC? Or ask Cyril Smith who served as MP? Ask Thatcher why she gave him a knighthood.

Exported diseases, like syphilis and gonorrhoea, telling me to be thankful for colonialism, as they built train tracks using my own ancestors as slaves. Then it only took them 70 years after leaving until the Americans came. Now there's no home, only a culture warped into an insignia of hate.

Now they want to say terrorism is the symptom of my religion or faith, as if terrorism isn't a cancer funded by

Reagan and the CIA. Then there's a president who hates people who submits to god and wear burqas, even though he's endorsed by the KKK.

The Berlin Wall collapsed in 1989, decades later bodies paralysed in prostration for the same fate for Palestine: West Bank an incomplete Odyssey, signing e-petitions like politicians aren't signing deals with devils, like Bush and Bin Laden didn't shake hands before 9/11; and from Grenfell to Suez there is no obituary, until it's a terror attack. On the topic of newspapers, who's heard of Daily Mail editor Paul Dacre? The paper that celebrated the election of Adolf Hitler. This isn't Breitbart, this is the truth I'm telling you.

And when I say the name Oswald, we're supposed to think about John F Kennedy, not to think about Britain's fascist leader 'Sir' Oswald Mosley. How the Daily Mail supported his Blackshirts?

Excuse me if I write poetry like blasphemy against governments, talking like a Pan-Africanist without the Nationalism, walking like the socialist without the radicalism, writing off my innocence. If we do not teach our children, society will, since the opposite of love isn't hate, it's indifference.

Haamid Sharif

PATCHWORK HUMAN

The sum of strangers:
equation of a 'what's left' afterlife,
amalgamation of all entities,
of all satellites,
all acquaintances,
of all not quite friends,
some rose-tinted strangers,
bus riders and villains,
your piercer, your preachers,
authors, foul mouthed teachers,
childhood myths and monsters,
close misdemeanours thanks to those ASBO kids.

Your one friend who will help you
scream "Hold tight Asznee!" in tears
in your Caucasian workplace,
'cause there's only like two of you
and it's theatre, so you Milly Rock in the wings
of ancient verse plays,
and there's a metaphor in there somewhere,
but your ribs are paper folding from laughing too much.

An ungovernable neighbour,

the first crush,

last pressed,

the homeless bloke who stole your baccy,

every heroic request from a potential dater,

a GASH rave and ill-fated decisions,

a chemical imbalance - no admin,

cured tendencies,

weekday disintegration,

nefarious dependency,

on a boy so fine his brown eyes sing Badu.

Best friend, enemies, in-betweens,

every bad memory,

the fires,

the floods,

hurricane Ivan and a lost plum tree.

Languages you don't speak,

creoles you definitely do,

every family member you don't know,

Genesis lyrics replaced every psalm you once knew,

every beach, water coconut and box dinner you ate,

every shit game of cricket

that your dad made you play.

The millennium, kids TV
the world worsening in a weekend,
the homophobes, the saboteurs, the socialists,
loneliness plays games of never have I ever
with my girlfriend.
New house mates all painters, brownie makers,
betraying your self-proclaimed introversion
straying to parties you hate,
Tequila being the less thespian version of self-immolation.

Terrible guidance counsellors, deadlines,
epiphanies, far too personal peer reviews,
all insults, thanks-yous, forgivings,
all favours, feigning care in the palm package expectancy
of a one night body-swap.

It's your partner now, your last gross hero,
it's 'Everything happens for a reason' -
a hapless proverb made to make you feel less awful
about the most human side of living,
the slap-dash mess that is being,
that is existing,
as though all tragedies find time
to gracefully fall into place,
like the misplaced purple rain of a poor Dionysus.

Originality is a fable, a man-made belief system
to make you and your tie dye feel better.
You are a patchwork human.
All that is tactile and powerful,
that is mild, gentle, overwhelmingly forgettable,
that is interesting and complex,
that is disgustingly simple.
Pastiche slices of psyche,
crafted pieces and portions of material memory,
our genius and misfortunes are hand-me-downs
to claim or denounce.

Billie Meredith

DREAMS

I only dreamed of getting on that train

and filling my wall with tickets.

When I was young I thought jumpers were goalposts, the

bins were wickets,

I thought the lamppost

outside my room was my personal moon.

I didn't know dreams were meant

to be forgotten in sleep,

with the pen I used to write these words,

I signed off Britain's post war bankruptcy note,

they should have used the daggers

I made from bread knives,

grenades from sock,

the trees that are blacksmith,

or created archers from school pencils

and elastic bands, you opted for Pickle Rick,

 when in my sleep I perform pilgrimages

in theatres, I am the left foot to a screamer by Pogba,

I am the Wimbledon to Roger Federer,

I am the Dragon to the Bruce Lee story,

dreams are more than a quiz show

or more than that tinder hook-up like Cilla Black, dreams

are real, dreams are Woody Guthrie

killing fascists with a guitar,

it's a conversation with the unconscious,

an interview with madness,

and you become the answer,

if I dream, I see me running on top of trains

like Mo Farah on a treadmill,

when I wake up: I see my train tickets on my wall.

Haamid Sharif

SHEDDING SNAKESKIN II

I'm tryna shed snakeskin head shaking, I can feel sweat
dripping from my nose into vantablack spacing—they lied
when they said making a bed to bury would fix it all.
I bleed venom into the sarcophagus and stare darkness
into black walls until colour creeps in and snakes massage
my limbs thick hisses morph into voices singing
  'Happiness is here if you want it'
    *S*tay with me, just that voice. I can't tell if I'm asleep
anymore, what's the difference between dreaming and
hallucinating when your eyes forget what reality tastes like.
I was running from light now I rest in oblivion.

I don't know if I was ready to meet God. The spitting
image of an evil half of my father showed me visions in
infinite darkness. I saw greed grow limbs and I saw—I saw
a seed, the seed grew into a chamber of self-destruction
and men entered by their own accord. I only ever saw an
entrance.
  If you listen closely you can almost hear their screams.
    They scare me they're watching me.

I can't get that image out of my head. I couldn't have
helped you, I didn't know how, I was too young, I was too
stupid.

happiness is here if you want it
I'm so scared. I read from the library of life.

The books of breath, the cinquains of sight, the code that
lies behind dark and light, the carvings in the black when
you close your eyes it says
'Everything you need is already here.'

But faith and fact sit on opposite sides of the coffee table.
When I sit inside the coffin, silence steps into the abyss,
darkness holds me dear sarcophagus, walls grow thinner
and perk their ears can't call me nigger it won't hurt me
here. I listen to God whisper
happiness is here if you want it
with the same hiss in the undertone sounds just like the
snakes—it's too dark to tell who said that.

Call me captain obvious but you can't die in a coffin or get
your life back. They lied when they told you coming here
fixes everything They lied when they told me coming here
would fix everything
don't be scared
I'M NOT - I'm just
I'm just lost and the monsters are all talking at the same
time as the pythons and anacondas and vipers comparing
spines and they all have different voices and I'm not

scared I'm just cold and I don't know where to go for warm clothes when it snows and I'm not home. I was bold when I left holding my chest told I was blessed but put to a test when I lost myself; a walking shell, cursed

told me find what's missing electric slide through hell shed my skin then swim through the mess I journeyed through trenches and explored their muddy depths I saw all that was left of the west and stuck around to make it better, with hopes to make the ghost forget to haunt me with my own regret, but only learnt I was powerless and they'd trouble me anyway.

I saw an alter horns and a candle set. I gazed at the crest on an ancient vest cocked, aimed and fired 12 sets of metal casted hollow lead at a bulletproof Baphomet. He smiled at my murderous intent and said:

'How far can stabbing get when the whole temple is under rubble?'

Hands full of holy water I sipped a quarter and spat at it. It hissed and fled, shedding its skin, leaving it and those words behind.

Damani Dennisur

ACT 2: PARENTALS

Happiness is here if you want it.

In the Janus faces of our prototypes,

whose sins we regurgitate and benevolence we swallow,

custodians of our identities,

homage to our precursors.

How do we write a coming of age story without their
influence, our fidelity?

Billie Meredith

WOLVES

Trust is a word I have
heard but seldom
understood

Your face concealed in
little red mother
hood

little was said
of how mother
should act

Lover always more
fairy tale
than fact

Have you ever seen two
wolves try to consume
each other's big bad?

I have.

Frankie Blaus

HINDSIGHT

Down
Me
Put
Senile
Go I- when: now it-
 about thinking
you're wine spiced over
promises made
You -when time in - back
thinking you're
But, fine, just be,
She'll -you'll tell - they'll-
Down Mother
Your tie lies
Cockerel and hands her in
holes
with Christ-like fighting fist
-be-
tonight
Down Mother
Your tie rites last in soaked
sponges from-
days, forty, sucked and-
Ghosts, foreign and

comatose
On herself: cured,
She - Down Mother,
Your tie 1941 in punctures:
bicycle for requiem wants,
She, living for? Are hymn
songs different?
Wants and plans
Funeral the seen.
She's Down Mother
Your tie: awake, she's
miracle a -
'It's treason' screams home,
'Go!' you when -
Over photos her turns lie
You - knows- she
Down Mother
Your tie- thighs rattling,
and kettles copying
fingernails,
Tangerine eyes,
Half-time with her,
Down
Mother your ---

Tie your Mother down,
Her, with half-time eyes,
Tangerine fingernails,
Copying kettles and rattling
thighs

Tie your Mother down,
She knows you lie,
turns her photos over when
you go home
Screams treason,
It's a miracle she's awake.
Tie your Mother down,
She's seen the funeral
plans,
and wants different songs,
hymns are for living:
she wants requiem for
bicycle punctures in 1941.

Tie your Mother down,
she cured herself on
comatose
and foreign ghosts,
and sucked forty days from
sponges soaked in last rites

Tie your Mother down
tonight,
she'll be fist-fighting Christ-
like
with holes in her hands
and Cockerel lies.

Tie your Mother down,
they'll tell you she'll be just
fine,
but you're thinking back in
time,
when you made promises
over spiced wine,

You're thinking about it
now:
'when I go senile put me
down'.

Roma Havers

AN ELEGY FOR MOTHER

I started dying yesterday Nan said you watch
over me I fastened your pictures over my bed because I
can't make her a liar
You still change with the days
Yesterday you were radiant, bright

Today my shroud tonight the aging glue holding my skull
together my father's monochromatic sausage of a finger
clicking through the fuzz
calling out past the cosmos then \\\ to the office
I was born with your name
in my mouth When I had more sense than years
I howled Did you ever hear that sound   ?

That's life

Looking at your face above my bed I learn every time what
it is
to grieve - I know
I will be sorry, killing you a second time
in forgetting how
to breathe

Frankie Blaus

SANDHOLE

Sensitive is what he said to me,

unworthy of my genealogy,

spine coded with A's C's and G's,

morphed by broken means:

homogen. Hide and seek,

I played myself for weeks.

Half him, I never wanted his skin,

I never wanted to be, him!

My body was painted by my mother,

she doesn't resemble me,

she said I reminded her of someone,

it wasn't him.

I accepted, I'd never be -

I'd never be like

this Black man tree height,

he seemed so high.

I isolated my individuality,

'cause I felt weak,

soft skin scars would open up and never heal,

I was an anomaly on a stool in the corner of my room,

back straight, I wouldn't move,

a recluse in my home,

refuge was 4 walls and a locked door,

overthinking reason, my heart beats

faster than I breathe,

I would chicken scratch my flesh 'til it bleeds,

I'd never sleep, boxed room cloaked by smoke,

protected by piles of clothes,

my head rests on pillows of Bedlam.

Jawara Tait

WHEN GASOLINE FREEZES

He laughed like he was shutting down.
apologies were
ulcered hands trembling.
A thrown match into a pool of petrol.

He stole
    and ran
        from his dying father.
An army man with
    legs tied together by the quick succession.

He was the speed limit
that made his wife crash her car.

I was the coat rack
   he knocked over
      instead of hitting her.

I stole.
Then turned away
from my dying father.
We're more like our parents
than we care to admit.
I became the twitch
in my mother's epileptic fit

Kayleigh Hicks

MY FUNCTIONING

There is so much of you
you half of me
    we of
        all hair
            all knowledge
                all chaos

        you are bird watching in a forest fire.

Man of all philosophy and no filigree
of no prayer
    of little hope in cynicism
        no warnings, constant rumblings
            manic intellectual

        alive but bored of living

All blues little grass
too alone too be mad anymore
    wrapped in grief
        wrapped in anger
            wrapped in

Manifestos of a Marxist no more Iliad can save you old
man and yet you still read

    all you do is read

My unfortunate - functioning.

Billie Meredith

DRIFTERS

He is midriffing the tide,
his head the knuckle of his fight,
he is walking,
like how Jesus would have had he too been
Father-figured-less, walking like portentousness,
every step there was less of him
spinal cord by
spinal cord by
spinal cord - so long with it.

Suddenly, childless,
his head the shadow of the moon,
bronze coined at the scalp,
he could have been faceless on the other side,
walking like there's nothing on his mind,
the tide: the Jekyll to his Hyde,
half-mannish half-oceanish,

and there: Salome served,
on the horizon platter,
obscenity-headed on my bledded sheet,
Have you ever seen your father walk into the sea?

Roma Havers

OUTRO

SHEDDING SNAKESKIN III

I was tryna shed snakeskin. I awaken and pop the cover
of the casket eyes adjust to fresh sunlight. I step outside
of a darkness that felt like it went on forever and into a
forest lights—the blood of the trees started pumping and
the balls of my feet drummed to the sound and those trees
whispered oh they sang hymns that could lift the dirt from
the ground and they lifted my soul from coffins and into
new life.

I can breathe again.

I can see again, spot the brink of life poking its head
over the edge of the end. I argued with solitude and
made a new friend when we shook hands and settled our
disputes. Now my shadow smiles at the paradigm of new
beginnings. It carved

'everything you need is already here' into my heart.

The words burn into the black I see when I close my eyes

before a time I learn to read preparing me for scary things

food for fear and flames of paranoia
hold me dear tell me happiness is here and know that
I want it and I'm reaching begging for reason
desperate for teachings
infiltrate my skull like slipping tincy wincy secrets through
aqueducts in coconuts

I'm learning the language of growing up
all important words stem from tongues of love
I close my eyes and read everything
I need breathe and look up

Happiness is here if you want it

Damani Dennisur

HAPPINESS

Ensemble

Happiness is here if you want it

                                   no need it!

          followed the crumbs home to find happiness is

fleeting in forest fires

          festivals of estrangement

bum on wooden stool

                back straight,

                don't move

                                  Happiness is here!

no here!

  My brother pointed to something

                    he couldn't reach

                      with his baby reins

        I dragged my mum to see

We have not reached the hard part yet

                hide and seek

                  with my dad

        until he fell asleep

        forehead fissured

                like a barcode and an

                    ovaltined mouth

happiness is longing
         for a time passed
sand between fingers
         and memory lapse
                        hands like an origami
                        fist folded in like role reversal
         the wet laugh-kiss
                  against the bathtub
                           rim

                  this is not the hard part

exposed at death's home
dead-zoned this epidemic
left dead bones

                        cherubs donning bling errors
scratching at basthets to the
tune of Ginsberg terrors
there is thirst in
         cut glass
         spit dust
                  Saliva doesn't taste the same
                           the voices took my breath away
                                    Happiness is here!

Trust us!

> words spin
>> like porcelain
> it's Morpheus
>> sleeping
>> with the maudlin

Happiness is here
> if you want it
>> No! need it!
>> followed the crumbs
> home to find happiness
> is fleeting
> longing for a time passed
sand between fingers
and memory lapse
Happiness is here somewhere

I'd bet my life on it.